Animal Neighbours

Hedgehog

Michael Leach

HODDER
Wayland

An imprint of Hodder Children's Books

Animal Neighbours

Titles in this series:

Badger • Deer • Fox • Hare • Hedgehog • Otter

Conceived and produced for Hodder Wayland by

Nutshell
MEDIA

Intergen House, 65–67 Western Road, Hove BN3 2JQ, UK
www.nutshellmedialtd.co.uk

Commissioning Editor: Vicky Brooker
Editor: Polly Goodman
Designer: Tim Mayer
Illustrator: Jackie Harland

Published in Great Britain in 2003 by Hodder Wayland, an imprint of Hodder Children's Books.

British Library Cataloguing in Publication Data
Leach, Michael, 1954 –
Hedgehog. – (Animal neighbours)
1. Hedgehogs – Juvenile literature
I. Title
599.3.'32

ISBN 0 7502 4167 5

Printed and bound in Hong Kong.

Hodder Children's Books
A division of Hodder Headline Limited
338 Euston Road, London NW1 3BH

Cover photograph: A hedgehog on some garden steps.
Title page: A hedgehog yawns and shows off its sharp teeth.

Picture acknowledgements
FLPA 6 (By Dembinsky), 16 (Mike J. Thomas), 19 (Foto Natura Stock), 21 (Albert Visage); Michael Leach
10, 11, 13, 15, 25, 28 right; Nature Picture Library 12 (Reijo Juurinen); NHPA *Cover* (Stephen Dalton),
Title page (Andy Rouse), 7 (Ashod Francis Papazian), 9, 14 (Daniel Heuchlin), 17 (Laurie Campbell), 22
(Daniel Heuchlin), 26 (Susanne Danegger), 28 bottom (Laurie Campbell); Oxford Scientific Films 8
(Tony Bomford), 20 (Mark Hamblin), 23 (Owen Newman), 24 (OSF), 28 top (Tony Bomford), 28 left
(Owen Newman); RSPCA Photolibrary 27 (Colin Seddon).

Contents

Meet the Hedgehog

Hedgehogs are small, nocturnal mammals covered in stiff, sharp spines. They live in many habitats across Europe, Asia and Africa, especially gardens, parks and farmland.

There are 17 species of hedgehog alive today. This book looks at the European hedgehog.

▲ **The red shading on this map shows where hedgehogs live in the world today.**

Spines

The hedgehog's spines were once soft hairs. They have evolved to become stiff, sharp spines, each 2–3 cm long, which protect the hedgehog from predators.

Legs

Hedgehogs have surprisingly long legs. They usually walk slowly, but a frightened hedgehog can run at a speed of 2 metres per second.

Feet

Each foot has five toes fitted with a sharp claw. The front feet are used to dig the earth while looking for insects. The back feet are used for grooming.

Underside

The hedgehog's underside is covered with thick, coarse hair instead of spines.

◀ The hedgehog is a third of the size of a domestic cat.

HEDGEHOG FACTS

The European hedgehog's scientific name is *Erinaceus europeaus*, which comes from the Latin words *erinaceus*, meaning 'hedgehog' and *europeaus*, meaning 'European'.

Male hedgehogs are known as boars, females as sows and young hedgehogs as hoglets.

Adult hedgehogs can be up to 30 cm long and weigh anything between 400–1,200 g. They are at their heaviest in the autumn, just before they hibernate. Males are usually slightly heavier than females.

Ears

Large ears give the hedgehog a good sense of hearing. The ears can swivel round to point in the direction of a sudden sound.

Eyes

Hedgehogs have small eyes that can spot movement very well, but they cannot see much detail and are quite short-sighted.

Nose

Hedgehogs have an excellent sense of smell, which helps them find food at night. Their strong, flexible snouts push through soil and grass to find insects.

Teeth

Hedgehogs have small, very sharp teeth that crush and slice off the hard outer parts of insects to reach the softer flesh inside.

The Hedgehog Family

Hedgehogs belong to a group of mammals known as insectivores. Most insectivores are small, nocturnal, live alone and feed mainly on invertebrates, especially insects. There are about 400 species of insectivores, from the very rare Pyrenean desman of the Pyrenees mountains, to more familiar animals such as hedgehogs, moles and shrews.

▼ The star-nosed mole uses the tentacles on its nose as feelers to find food underground.

The first hedgehogs appeared around 30 million years ago. Since then, many species have evolved and become extinct, including a giant hedgehog known as *Deinogalerix*. This was the size of a badger and became extinct about 5 million years ago.

▲ The desert hedgehog lives in dry areas of North Africa. It gets water from its prey of insects, worms and small mammals.

There are 12 species of true hedgehogs as well as five distant cousins, known as moon rats. Moon rats have thick hair instead of spines.

Hedgehogs around the world have adapted to living in different habitats. The desert hedgehog from the Sahara Desert builds an underground den to avoid the hot sun. The Asian long-eared hedgehog also builds an underground den. The den is a long tunnel. If a predator approaches, the hedgehog escapes into the tunnel instead of rolling into a ball.

Birth and Growing Up

As a pregnant female hedgehog gets ready to give birth, she builds a large, round nest of grass and leaves. The nest is usually hidden underneath dead wood, or in thick undergrowth.

At birth, new-born hoglets are pink, blind and completely helpless. They are born with tiny spines, but the spines are trapped under a layer of thin skin to stop them damaging the sow during birth.

If the den is disturbed in any way during the first few days after birth, the sow usually eats her young. At this age, the hoglets would not survive being moved.

▲ **The spines of this new-born hedgehog are tucked away under its skin.**

8

HOGLETS

New-born hoglets are about 65 mm long and weigh about 15 g.

Female hedgehogs normally give birth to a litter of four or five young hoglets.

At 24 hours old, each hoglet has around 100 white spines. During the following day a set of thicker, darker spines appear. About 10 days after birth, the first hairs begin to grow.

▲ This hoglet is only 2 days old but already it has a covering of sharp spines.

By eating them, the mother gains the strength to breed again. If the hoglets are over a week old when danger threatens, their mother will carry them to a new den in her mouth.

The mother stays with her litter during the day, suckling them frequently. During the night, she goes out to find food. While she is away, the hoglets sometimes produce high-pitched squeals of hunger.

Early days

The hoglets' eyes do not open fully until they are about 2 weeks old, although the eyelids will roll up before this if they are frightened or disturbed. Hoglets are very afraid of loud noises and will curl up at the slightest sound outside the nest.

At 3 weeks old, the hoglets leave the den for the first time. They follow their mother closely as she searches for food, picking up small insects that she uncovers with her snout. They quickly learn what to eat and how to use their sense of smell to find their own food.

▲ Once the hoglet has a thick covering of spines, fleas and mites will move across from its mother to live in its spines.

The hoglets drink their mother's milk until they are about 5 weeks old, when she will begin to drive them away. Eventually, the mother will bite her young if they continue to try to suckle. It is time for the young hedgehogs to leave.

▼ Hoglets recognise their mother by her scent.

COAT OF ARMOUR

A fully grown hedgehog has up to 7,000 spines. Each spine has its own tiny set of muscles, which are used to lower or raise the spine. The end of each spine is anchored under the skin in a large, rounded shape. This holds the spine in place and stops it puncturing the hedgehog's body. A single spine lasts for about two years, before dropping out and being replaced by a new one.

Habitat

After leaving its mother, each hedgehog wanders off in search of its own territory. Most hedgehogs never move more than 2 kilometres from the place they were born. Each hedgehog must find an area of thick vegetation where they can sleep on summer days and hibernate in winter.

▼ Hedgehogs often drink from garden ponds. They use their long tongues to lap up the water.

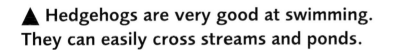

▲ **Hedgehogs are very good at swimming. They can easily cross streams and ponds.**

Hedgehogs do not like dense woodlands. They prefer habitats that are a mixture of trees, shrubs and grass. Here they can feed on open grassland at night and then find somewhere to hide during the day. Farmland, parks and gardens are excellent places to look for hedgehogs.

Hedgehogs live alone and are completely nocturnal. They spend their days sleeping in deep undergrowth or beneath piles of leaves. Just after sunset, they wake for a night of hunting. They must always find somewhere safe to hide again before dawn.

TERRITORY

Sows have territories of about 12 hectares.

Boar territories can be up to 35 hectares.

Hedgehogs do not fight over territory. If the food supply is good, several hedgehogs will live close together, but they are solitary animals that always avoid each other at night.

Prickly defences

The hedgehog's spines are an excellent method of self-defence. If a fox, badger or other predator approaches, the hedgehog automatically rolls itself into a prickly ball, with its head hidden safely in the centre. This action is very fast and is controlled by a powerful muscle that wraps around the sides of the hedgehog, just beneath the skin. At the same time, smaller muscles move the spines and make them stick out at different angles.

▼ Foxes are attracted by the scent of hedgehogs, but they quickly leave when they feel the spines.

▲ When a hedgehog rolls up, its sensitive eyes and nose are tucked deep inside the spines, away from danger.

The hedgehog also uses its prickly coat to avoid injury. It can climb over obstacles such as fences and roll down the other side as a ball, using its spines to absorb the shock.

ROMAN HEDGEHOGS

About 2,000 years ago, the Romans dried hedgehog skins and used the spines to comb sheep wool. The wool was then spun and woven into clothing. A popular Roman myth was that hedgehogs collected apples to eat by spearing them on their spines!

The grey-brown spines of a hedgehog provide perfect camouflage for an animal that comes out at night. Hedgehogs are very difficult to see in the dark, although they are often heard as they loudly sniff the ground searching for food.

Hibernation

Most invertebrates, such as worms and insects, disappear in the winter. So every autumn, to avoid starvation, hedgehogs have to find somewhere safe to sleep until their food supply returns the following spring. This is called hibernation.

At the end of the summer, hedgehogs spend many weeks eating as much as possible. In October or November, each hedgehog builds a hibernation den. They collect lots of leaves and pack them tightly together in a large mound under a thick hedgerow, or beneath a pile of dead branches. Hedgehogs in urban habitats often build their dens under garden sheds.

▼ A hibernating hedgehog appears to be completely dead.

This hedgehog is ▶ just leaving its hibernation den inside a rotten log.

HEARTBEAT AND TEMPERATURE

When it hibernates, the hedgehog's heart rate slows down from 150 to just 18 beats a minute. Its body temperature drops from 34 °C to as low as 4 °C. This is just enough to keep the hedgehog alive. A human can pick up a hibernating hedgehog and it will not wake. But even in deep hibernation, the hedgehog's spines will raise when it is disturbed or hears a loud noise.

Inside the den, the hedgehog is protected against the worst of the winter weather and falls into a very deep sleep.

The hedgehog will not sleep for the whole winter. Most hedgehogs wake up and move to a new den at least once before the spring arrives. On warm winter days, hedgehogs sometimes wake, leave the den and look around for food. But they always go back to sleep when the temperature drops again at night.

Food

Hedgehogs feed mainly on earthworms, but they will eat almost any invertebrate, including beetles, slugs and even snakes. They will feed on dead animals, eggs and chicks, and they sometimes even eat grass, seeds and soft fruit.

▼ Only badgers prey on adult hedgehogs. Hoglets are eaten by owls and foxes. (The illustrations are not to scale.)

Hedgehog food chain

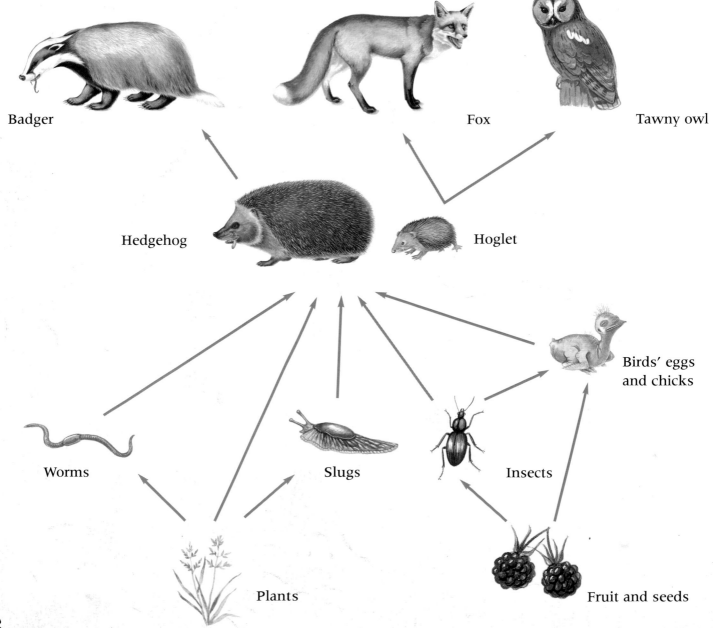

Badger

Fox

Tawny owl

Hedgehog

Hoglet

Birds' eggs and chicks

Worms

Slugs

Insects

Plants

Fruit and seeds

▲ Each hedgehog eats about 70 grams of food in a single night.

MILK THIEVES?

Hedgehogs were once believed to steal milk from sleeping cows at night. In 1566 in England, there was a reward of 3 pence for anyone catching a hedgehog milking a cow! Hedgehogs are often found in fields near cows because they eat the insects that live in and around cow dung.

Hedgehogs pick up most of their prey in their mouth, but some need special treatment. Slugs are covered with a thick mucous that stops them drying out and helps them slide easily over the ground. Hedgehogs do not like the taste of this slime, so before they eat a slug, they step on it and roll it around the ground to remove the unpleasant mucous.

Occasionally, hedgehogs eat small mammals such as voles. They are not fast enough to catch the adult voles, so they usually only take the young that they find in nests on the ground.

Gardeners' friends

Hedgehogs are very useful to gardeners because they eat many of the small pests that destroy flowers and vegetables. Many people try to attract hedgehogs into gardens by leaving out bread and milk. Hedgehogs eagerly eat this meal, but it can make them ill because they cannot easily digest cows' milk. Tinned dog food is a much better meal to give a hedgehog.

Hedgehogs living on coasts regularly visit beaches at night to search for small animals stranded on the sand by a high tide. They investigate piles of seaweed with their snouts. Probing and sniffing, they feed on the tiny crabs and other creatures hiding inside.

▼ Dog food is good for hedgehogs, particularly in the autumn, when they need to put on weight ready for hibernation.

During the autumn, hedgehogs must eat as much as possible to build up their body weight ready for winter. Hedgehogs born late in the year are unlikely to survive because they do not have the thick layer of fat needed to take them through hibernation. At the start of winter, a hedgehog must weigh at least 450 grams to have any chance of living through the next five months without food.

▲ The hedgehog's spines protect it against the adder's poisonous bite. Hedgehogs are one of the few animals that eat adders.

21

Finding a Mate

By the time they are one year old, hedgehogs are ready to breed. When they first come out from hibernation in the spring, hedgehogs spend about a month eating to build up their weight after the long winter. Then they begin to look for a mate.

▼ A nest of quail's eggs is a welcome treat to a hungry hedgehog.

Male hedgehogs find a female by following her scent. He walks around her in circles at first until she allows him to mate. This may take a long time because the sow often raises her spines and bites the boar when he gets too close. The boar leaves after mating and takes no part in rearing the young. About four weeks after mating, the hoglets are born.

If the first litter appears early in the year, the sow may mate again and produce more young in the summer. Sows will also breed again if their young are eaten by predators.

▲ **The sow eventually allows the boar to mate.**

23

Threats

The hedgehog's spiny coat protects it against most predators. Even medium-size hunters such as stoats and foxes often give up once they have been stabbed in the nose. However, hedgehogs are sometimes killed by pet dogs. The bigger breeds have much longer teeth than foxes, and can easily bite through the thick layer of spines.

HEDGEHOG DINNER

Hundreds of hedgehog bones have been found in ancient fires all over Europe, which suggests that people living in the Stone Age used to eat hedgehogs. At that time, people only had simple weapons, so larger animals were harder to kill. The hedgehog must have been a very important source of meat.

◀ Labradors and other large dog breeds can kill hedgehogs, but not without receiving a few scratches from the sharp spines.

The hedgehog's biggest killer is road traffic. A hedgehog crossing a road automatically rolls into a tight ball when it hears the sound of an approaching car. This is a good method of self-defence when faced with a fox, but useless when the enemy is half a tonne of steel moving at 80 kilometres per hour. However, some hedgehogs may be learning new tricks. Scientists believe that hedgehogs are now starting to run, instead of roll up, when they hear a car approaching.

▲ Every year thousands of hedgehogs die while crossing roads.

◀ Piles of dead leaves like this one make favourite hibernation dens for hedgehogs.

Accidental deaths

People accidentally kill hedgehogs in many different ways. In the autumn, hedgehogs like to make their hibernation dens under piles of dead leaves, which are raked up in parks and gardens. If the leaves are moved or built into a bonfire, the hedgehog beneath can be killed. If the hedgehog is just asleep, it will usually move at the first smell of fire. But if it is hibernating, it will not wake up in time. The hedgehog's camouflage makes it almost impossible to see under a pile of dead leaves or wood.

Garden machinery such as hedge strimmers and lawnmowers can accidentally kill or injure hibernating hedgehogs. Some hedgehogs drown in steep-sided ponds or swimming pools. If they go to a pool to drink, it is easy to fall in and not get out again. Other hedgehogs die after eating poisons left out by farmers or gardeners to kill pests such as slugs and mice.

LIFESPAN

Hedgehogs can live up to the age of 6 years in the wild, although very few ever reach this age. The average lifespan is 2 years.

The first six months of a hedgehog's life are the most dangerous. Less than half the hedgehogs born every year will survive until the age of one.

◀ Hedgehogs are sometimes injured by litter. This hedgehog was trying to reach the bottom of the cat-food tin when it got stuck.

Hedgehog Life Cycle

1 The new-born hoglet is pink, blind and completely helpless. It is just 65 mm long.

2 At 2 weeks old, the hoglet opens its eyes for the first time.

5 After the age of one, the hedgehog mates and produces young.

4 In the autumn, the hedgehog goes into hibernation for the first time.

3 At 6 weeks old, the young hedgehog leaves its mother and becomes independent.

Hedgehog Clues

Look out for the following clues to help you find signs of a hedgehog:

Dens
Hedgehogs make their sleeping dens in thick vegetation, such as long grass, hedgerows or bushes. The dens are easier to find in the winter, when the vegetation dies away. Hibernation dens are more difficult to find. They are hidden deep under piles of wood or dead leaves, and often under garden sheds. If you find a den, do not disturb the hedgehog inside. The den may contain a sow with young. If she is frightened, she could abandon or even eat the hoglets.

Sniffs and snuffles
Hedgehogs are very noisy feeders. They constantly produce a series of loud, short sniffs when they are eating, which can be heard from a long way away. But it is very difficult to pinpoint where their sounds come from, so hedgehogs are more often heard than seen.

Footprints
The hedgehog's footprint shows its five toes, each ending with a sharp claw. Rats and water voles leave similar prints, but the hedgehog's footprints are slightly bigger.

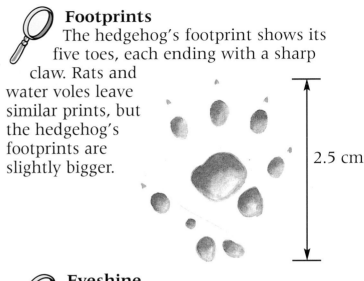

2.5 cm

Eyeshine
Like all nocturnal mammals, hedgehogs have eyes that reflect bright light. If you shine torchlight in a garden or park at night, it will bounce off a hedgehog's eyes and can be seen as two bright-red spots glowing in the darkness. The reflections are close together and are always at ground level.

Droppings
Hedgehog droppings are long, black and glossy. They contain the remains of insects, and shiny beetle wings are often clearly visible in the droppings.

3–4 cm

Glossary

boar A male hedgehog. The males of pigs and badgers are also called boars.

camouflage The colour or pattern of some animals that helps them blend in with their surroundings and makes them hard to see.

digest To break down food in the stomach so the body can absorb its energy.

evolved Developed and changed over millions of years.

extinct An animal species that has completely died out.

grooming Cleaning the body.

habitat The area where an animal or plant naturally lives.

hedgerow A row of plants that are specially planted close together to make a thick, living fence.

hibernate To enter a deep sleep that lasts most of the winter.

insectivore An animal that eats insects.

invertebrates Animals that do not have a backbone.

litter A group of young animals born at the same time from the same mother.

mucous A protective thick and sticky liquid.

nocturnal An animal that sleeps during the day and is active at night.

predator A hunting animal that kills and eats other animals.

prey An animal that is killed and eaten by other animals.

short-sighted Eyesight that can only see things that are very close.

solitary An animal that lives alone.

sow A female hedgehog. The females of pigs and badgers are also called sows.

suckle When a mother allows her young to drink milk from her teats.

territory An area that an animal or group of animals defends against others of the same species.

urban A habitat in a town or city.

Finding Out More

Other books to read

Animal Sanctuary by John Bryant (Open Gate Press, 1999)

Animal Young: Mammals by Rod Theodorou (Heinemann, 1999)

Classification: Animal Kingdom by Kate Whyman (Hodder Wayland, 2000)

Collins Nature Guides: Garden Wildlife of Britain and Europe by Michael Chinery (Collins Natural History, 1997)

The Giant Book of Creatures of the Night by Jim Pipe (Watts, 1998)

Hedgehogs by Pat Morris and Guy Troughton (Whittet Books, 1995)

Life Cycles: Cats and Other Mammals by Sally Morgan (Belitha, 2001)

Living with Urban Wildlife by John Bryant (Open Gate Press, 2002)

Moles and Hedgehogs by Sara Swan Miller (Franklin Watts, 2000)

New Encyclopedia of Mammals by David Macdonald (OUP, 2001)

The Wayland Book of Common British Mammals by Shirley Thompson (Hodder, 2000)

What's the Difference?: Mammals by Stephen Savage (Hodder Wayland, 1998)

Wild Britain: Woodlands, Parks & Gardens, Meadows by R. & L. Spilsbury (Heinemann, 2000)

Organisations to contact

British Hedgehog Preservation Society
Hedgehog House, Dhustone, Ludlow, Shropshire SY8 3PL
Tel. 01584 890801
www.software-technics.co.uk/bhps

Countryside Foundation for Education
PO Box 8, Hebden Bridge HX7 5YJ
www.countrysidefoundation.org.uk
Training and teaching materials to help people understand the countryside and its problems.

English Nature
Northminster House, Peterborough, Cambridgeshire PE1 1UA
Tel. 01733 455000
www.englishnature.org.uk

The Mammal Society
15 Cloisters House, 8 Battersea Park Road, London SW8 4BG
www.mammal.org.uk
Promotes the study and conservation of British mammals.

Wildlife Watch
National Office, The Kiln, Waterside, Mather Road, Newark NG24 1WT
www.wildlifetrusts.org
The junior branch of the Wildlife Trusts, a network of local Wildlife Trusts caring for nearly 2,500 nature reserves, from rugged coastline to urban wildlife havens, protecting a huge number of habitats and species.

Index

Page numbers in **bold** refer to a photograph or illustration.